MW00412367

HARD-CORE
IDOLATRY

FACING THE FACTS

HARD-CORE IDOLATRY

FACING THE FACTS

C. PETER WAGNER

WAGNER
PUBLICATIONS

Unless otherwise indicated, all Scripture quotations are from *The New King James Version.* Copyright © 1979, 1980, 1982, Thomas Nelson, Inc. Used by permission.

The Holy Bible: New International Version (NIV), copyright © 1973, 1978, 1984 by International Bible Society. All rights reserved.

Hard-Core Idolatry: Facing the Facts
Copyright © 1999, 2001 by C. Peter Wagner
ISBN 1-58502-020-6
Revised Edition

Published by
Wagner Publications
11005 N. Highway 83
Colorado Springs, CO 80921
www.wagnerpublications.org

Cover design by
Hala Saad
Vision Communications
711 Lowell Street
Dallas, Texas 75214
(214) 827-0620

Interior design by
Rebecca Sytsema

Printed in the United States of America. All rights reserved under International Copyright Law. Contents and/or cover may not be reproduced in whole or in part without the express written consent of the publisher.

Rights for publishing this book in other languages are contracted by Gospel Literature International (GLINT). GLINT also provides technical help for the adaptation, translation, and publishing of Bible study resources and books in scores of languages worldwide. For further information, contact GLINT, P.O. Box 4060, Ontario, CA 91761-1003, USA. You may also send e-mail to glintint@aol.com, or visit their web site at www.glint.org.

2 3 4 5 6 7 8 9   06 05 04 03 02 01

TABLE OF CONTENTS

CHAPTER ONE

IDOLATRY TODAY: LET'S GET SERIOUS

In my almost fifty years of walking the Christian walk, I have heard very few sermons on idolatry—*hard-core* idolatry, that is. The word "idolatry" is, in fact, used quite frequently by Christian leaders, but, unfortunately, a very small percentage of them are talking about idolatry the way the Bible talks about it. The Bible does have a great deal to say about blatant idolatry, and I believe we need to understand and deal with it much more seriously than we have been.

Today is Different

Why do we need to be more aware of idolatry? It would be difficult to pinpoint any era since the Protestant Reformation in which the church as a whole has been more overtly engaged in spiritual warfare on the higher levels than we are today. We live in a time in which God is not only calling His people to engage in more intense spiritual warfare than any of us can remember, but He is also providing His people with powerful spiritual equipment that we have not been accustomed to. Ten years ago, terms such as "strategic-level spiritual warfare," "spiritual mapping," "identificational repentance," "territorial commitment," and "city transformation" were not part of our vocabulary. But today we have been blessed with a whole library of books covering these vital subjects, and large numbers of Christians are on the front lines putting these weapons of warfare into practice.

The purpose of this new spiritual equipment is to win lost people to Jesus Christ. Jesus came to "seek and to save that which was lost." His last words spoken on the face of

---

If we are ignorant of Satan's devices, we make ourselves unnecessarily vulnerable for him to take advantage of us.

---

this earth were what we now call the Great Commission: "You shall receive power when the Holy Spirit has come upon you; and you shall be witnesses to Me in Jerusalem, and in all Judea and Samaria, and to the end of the earth" (Acts 1:8). To a large extent, God's people have been faithful in moving in the power of the Holy Spirit and advancing the Kingdom of God with unprecedented speed in the past decade.

For example, at the beginning of the 1990s there were

1,739 significantly large unreached people groups, mostly in the 10/40 Window. Massive prayer was mobilized for them, to the extent of seeing 50 million believers praying for the same people group on the same day in an initiative called Praying Through the Window. Largely as a result of this, at this writing only 500 of those unreached people groups still do not have an initial church planting movement, and that number continues to shrink at a rapid rate.

Today is truly different.

The Devil Is Furious!

However, through all of this, the spiritual warfare and the counterattacks of Satan have become much more intense. This is to be expected. We are probably seeing a literal enactment of Revelation 12:12: "The devil has come down to you, having great wrath, because he knows that he has a short time." He is furious because kingdoms and people groups in which he has enjoyed free reign for millennia are now bursting open to the light of the gospel. He is incensed that his assigned demonic principalities are losing their grip on China and Nepal and Northern India and Thailand and Latin America and the Philippines, just to name a few. With his back to the wall, so to speak, Satan is ready to risk everything to stem the tide of the gospel.

One of our duties as Christians is to be aware of what Satan is up to. Paul writes, "Lest Satan should take advantage of us . . . we are not ignorant of his devices" (2 Cor. 2:11). Turning that around, it becomes clear that *if* we are ignorant of Satan's devices, we make ourselves unnecessarily vulnerable for him to take advantage of us. He attacks us on at least two fronts. The first is an attempt to weaken us or destroy us as individuals. Soldiers who end up in the hospital for one rea-son or another are a detriment, rather than a help, for winning the battle. Satan attacks us through the world, the flesh, and the devil. He tries to discourage us, to make us sick, to lead us into accidents, to wound us through broken relationships, to abuse our bodies through unwise substances, to puncture our self-esteem, to entice us to look at or listen to things that in-vite evil, to weaken us emotionally by attacking our family members, and on and on.

One of the devices Satan frequently uses to accomplish these purposes and to put the soldiers of God into the hospi-tal is to resurrect our "old man" who should have been crucified with Christ (see Rom. 6:6). Another is to afflict us with some kind of curse. Another is to find openings through which he can assign demons to afflict us. And another is to seduce us into seeking supernatural power from sources other than God.

Satan's Plan A and Plan B

If Satan fails at all of the above (which he should if we are living lives of radical holiness, if we are fully committed to God, and if we are protected with a shield of intercessory prayer), he will often switch to a second front. He will try to deceive us into foggy thinking about the task of reaching the lost, and thereby reduce our effectiveness in reaching them for Christ. His Plan A is usually to try to enshroud us with a pervasive apathy toward the lost. If he succeeds here, not much more needs to be done because we are no longer a threat to him. But if Satan's Plan A fails, and if we do maintain a burning passion for finding the lost sheep, his Plan B often comes into play. He tries to cloud our thinking so that we ignore or misunderstand certain vital aspects of the job God has sent us to do.

CHAPTER TWO

TRIVIALIZING
IDOLATRY

In this book I want to address just one of the many approaches that Satan takes to fog our thinking, namely *trivializing idolatry.* I could do similar essays on some of Satan's other attempts to keep us off track such as misdefining evangelism, confusing the evangelistic and cultural mandates, underestimating the cost of discipleship, prioritizing truth over mercy, ministry in word but not in deed, cultural insensitivity, indifference to effective follow up, mismatching the harvest force to the harvest field, fear of confronting the demonic realm, sending in ground troops without first controlling the air space, ignorance of spiritual mapping, despair of ever living a holy life, and the like. But this time I am focusing especially on our serious misunderstanding of idolatry.

Particularly among those of us from Western, traditionally Christian cultures, the enemy has succeeded in implanting two unfortunate mindsets relating to idolatry. The first is that worshiping idols is neither widespread nor serious since idols have no substance other than being pieces of wood or stone or whatever. The second potentially debilitating mindset is that it is legitimate to refer to just about any habitual sin a person commits as "idolatry." Both of these tend to trivialize idolatry and thereby weaken the body of Christ. They probably don't reduce our evangelistic effectiveness to zero, but they do have an effect similar to a professional football team trying to win a game with ten instead of eleven players on the field.

What Is Idolatry?

Idolatry is worshiping, serving, pledging allegiance to, doing acts of obeisance to, paying homage to, forming alliances with, making covenants with, seeking power from, or in any other way exalting any supernatural being other than God. The supernatural beings refer to angels, cherubim, seraphim, Satan, principalities, powers, deities, territorial spirits, goddesses, and demonic beings on any other level.

The Sin That God Hates the Most

God hates all sin, but obviously some sins are worse than others. I do not believe that the Ten Commandments are necessarily listed in the order of their severity, but I do think that the first two commandments are first on the list because they are the sins that God hates the most. Evidence throughout other parts of Scripture suggests this very strongly, as we shall see. Here are the first two commandments from Exodus

20:3-5:

1. You shall have no other gods before Me.

2. You shall not make for yourself any carved image, or any likeness of anything that is in heaven above, or that is in the earth beneath, or that is in the water under the earth; you shall not bow down to them nor serve them.

These commandments are what idolatry is all about. It is about worshiping beings in the invisible world, which often

---

Physical adultery is bad enough, but in God's value system spiritual adultery, which we call idolatry, is much worse!

---

leads to a special recognition of tangible objects ("carved images" or idols), in the visible world. What you see in the visible world is a person bowing down or making a sacrifice or burning incense either to an image of some kind or to a feature of creation like the sun, a mountain, a rock, or a river. What is actually taking place behind the scenes is a spiritual transaction with one or more spirit beings in the invisible world. This is what I am calling "hard-core idolatry."

Joshua's Last Word

At the end of Joshua's career, just before he died at 110 years of age, he called the people of Israel together and gave them his parting words. His heart's desire was that, when he was gone, the people would prosper and enjoy God's best for them. So what were his final instructions? At this crucial point in history, Joshua did not admonish the people to abstain from adultery, stealing, murder, or taking the Lord's name in vain. He did not remind them to keep the Sabbath or to honor their parents. Not that any of these things was unimportant—but none of them was, at the time, *the most* important. Joshua said, "Fear the Lord, serve Him in sincerity and in truth, and put away the gods which your fathers served on the other side of the River and in Egypt" (Josh. 24:14). That was the most important instruction he could leave.

So there would be no misunderstanding, Joshua went into more detail. If they ever went into the territory of another nation, he said:

♦ You shall not make mention of the name of their gods;

♦ Nor cause anyone to swear by them;

♦ Nor serve them;

♦ Nor bow down to them (see Josh. 23:7).

Bottom line: "Choose for yourselves this day whom you will serve . . . As for me and my house, we will serve the Lord" (Josh. 24:15). The number one issue for Joshua was hard-core idolatry.

Idolatry Caused the Babylonian Captivity

Unfortunately, the children of Israel, through most of their generations, chose not to follow Joshua's advice nor to obey the first two commandments. With the exception of some relatively short times of revival, idolatry crept in and persisted until God could no longer withhold judgment. The punishment was the Babylonian captivity, as prophesied by Jeremiah: "This whole land shall be a desolation and an astonishment, and these nations shall serve the king of Babylon seventy years" (Jer. 25:11).

I mention this because the most detailed and extensive treatment of idolatry in the Bible is found in the first nineteen chapters of Jeremiah. If anyone doubts that this is the sin that God hates the most, they need only to read these chapters. For example:

- ♦ "I will utter My judgments against them concerning all their wickedness, because they have forsaken Me, burned incense to other gods, and worshiped the works of their own hands" (Jer. 1:16).

- ♦ "You said, 'I will not transgress,' when on every high hill and under every green tree, you lay down playing the harlot" (Jer. 2:20).

- ♦ "She has committed adultery with stones and trees . . . and [you] have scattered your charms to alien deities under every green tree" (Jer. 3:9,13).

- ♦ "Just as you have forsaken Me and served foreign gods in your land, so you shall serve aliens in a land that is not yours" (Jer. 5:19).

- ♦ "The children gather wood, the fathers kindle the fire, and the women knead their dough to make cakes for the queen of heaven . . . that they may provoke Me to anger" (Jer. 7:18).

♦ "Why has the Lord pronounced all this great disaster against us? Or what is our iniquity? Or what is our sin that we have committed against the Lord our God?" . . . "'Because your fathers have forsaken Me,' says the Lord; 'They have walked after other gods and have served them and worshiped them, and have forsaken Me and not kept My law'" (Jer. 16:10-11).

Enough said. However, it should be mentioned that since the punishment of the Babylonian captivity, hard-core idolatry has not returned as a generalized problem among the Jews. They learned a bitter lesson.

Idolatry and Adultery

Did you notice how many times idolatry was compared to adultery in Jeremiah? It is because God is a jealous God and this metaphor communicates with most people. Let's understand what it means by playing out a hypothetical scenario:

You come home from work for dinner, but your wife isn't there like she usually is. You make some phone calls, but you cannot locate her. You spend a sleepless night worrying about her. In the morning she comes in and says, "Darling, you know the man who has been cutting my hair? He's a wonderful man, and he invited me to go to his apartment and spend the night with him. We had a very nice time. He says he only wants me to go there once a month, so don't worry—I'll still spend most of my time with you!"

Guaranteed—you would be a jealous man! But this is ex-

actly how God feels when Christian people—His bride—
worship, serve, or ask favors from other spiritual beings.
Physical adultery is bad enough, but in God's value system
spiritual adultery, which we call idolatry, is much worse!

CHAPTER THREE

Soft-Core Idolatry

As I mentioned earlier, Christian leaders use the word "idolatry" frequently. However, few of them mean the kind of idolatry that we have been looking at, namely hard-core idolatry. Idolatry to them is any pattern in our lives which might keep us from knowing God or from being fully committed to God.

Before I share my thoughts on why this happens, we should recognize that the Bible does not use the word "idolatry" very much. "Idolatry" and its derivatives ("idolater(s)," idolatries," "idolatrous") appear only 18 times in the New King James Bible. It is, therefore, understandable that a certain amount of fuzziness could well creep into our thinking on the subject.

The "Sin of the Month"

Why is it that pastors have a tendency to refer to what we might call "the sin of the month" as "idolatry"? It is because they know from the Scriptures how much God hates idolatry and how He will punish those who persist in committing idolatry. One of the best ways that pastors can impress people with the severity of the sin of the month is by labeling it "idolatry." Their point is that God hates that sin, whatever it may be, and that He will punish those who persist in it. It is a good thought, emerging from a good motive. But few pastors realize that by calling the sin of the month "idolatry," they are trivializing real idolatry.

Underlying this kind of preaching is the fact that few Western pastors have had first-hand experience with hard-core idolatry. I am quoting this from a recent publication that does not need to be identified. The author is telling how we must prepare for revival, and says (among other things) that: "You must recognize and overcome idolatry. Many of us think in terms of serving foreign gods. However, in ministry settings, the most common form of idolatry is that of congregations who idolize their ministers." This author's sin of the month is thinking too much of one's pastor. I have kept a file of other sins that are actually referred to as "idolatry" in publications: putting children or spouse ahead of God, giving too much time and energy to Christian ministry, television, personal pleasures, too much food, books signed by their author, building a building. You could add numerous others to the list. How many times, for example, have you heard professional football referred to as "idolatry?"

I am realistic enough to recognize that many pastors

will persist in using "idolatry" to condemn sins in general. And they have a certain point, because they are saying that we should not allow anything in our lives that could possibly take priority over knowing and serving God. But let's recognize that, if we use the word "idolatry" for any persistent sin which might interrupt our ideal relationship to God, it is essentially *soft-core* idolatry. It is not good, but to get back to the analogy of adultery, this would relate to hard-core idolatry as a passionate kiss would relate to sexual intercourse. Both are wrong outside of marriage, but they cannot be equated.

To show that ordinary works of the flesh are sin, but they are not idolatry, let's look at the Bible. In 1 Corinthians 5, Paul exhorts Christians not to keep company with fellow believers who are: sexually immoral, covetous, extortioners, or drunkards, or revilers, *or idolaters* (see 1 Cor. 5:10,11). Implication: drunkenness or reviling or immorality or extortion are bad sins, but they are something other than idolatry. Or consider Colossians 3:5: "Therefore put to death your members which are on the earth: fornication, uncleanness, passion, evil desire, and covetousness, which is idolatry."

Covetousness is Hard-Core Idolatry

The only sin which could appear to be a sin of the flesh and which is equated with idolatry in biblical lists like these is covetousness. Ephesians 5:5 says, "For this you know, that no fornicator, unclean person, nor covetous man, *who is an idolater*, has any inheritance in the kingdom of Christ and God." Fornicators are not necessarily idolaters, but covetous people are. Why is this? There is a good reason. It is because covetousness, unlike many other sins, is hard-core idolatry.

Covetousness is allegiance to a false god named Mammon. *Mamona* is an Aramaic term for wealth. First century rabbis considered *Mamona* a demonic being and a rival of God. That is why the NIV translated Jesus' words in Luke 16:13: "You cannot serve both God and Money [Mammon]." It is correct to capitalize "Money" or "Mammon" because it is a proper name. Mammon is a person, not a thing or an urge or an attitude. Translations that do not capitalize Mammon lose some of the force of the original because undoubtedly the translators were not aware of what New Testament scholars now affirm.[1] When Jesus mentioned Mammon, it was in the context of not being able to serve two masters. Serving any supernatural master in the demonic world, like Mammon, is hard-core idolatry.

Idols in the Heart

I once heard a preacher use Ezekiel 14:4 to justify calling sins of the flesh "idolatry." It speaks of "everyone of the house of Israel who sets up his idols in his heart, and puts before him what causes him to stumble into iniquity. . ." The context of this passage, however, is not soft-core idolatry, but hard-core idolatry. Just before that passage, Ezekiel speaks of "women who sew magic charms on their sleeves and make veils for the heads of people of every height to hunt souls" (Ezek. 13:18). And just after that passage we read of those who "made for yourself male images and played the harlot with them." (Ezek. 16:17); and "you have slain My children and offered them up to them by causing them to pass through the fire" (Ezek. 16:21); and "you also built for yourself a shrine, and made a high place for yourself in every street" (Ezek. 16:24).

The idolatry of Israel was the real thing!

Worshiping Human Beings

Is giving excessive honor to a human being hard-core or soft-core idolatry? It can be either, depending on whether the honor crosses the line to become actual worship. Godly human beings recognize the difference, and they do not accept worship. For example, when Peter went into the house of Cornelius, Acts says, "Cornelius met him and fell down at his feet and worshiped him" (Acts 10:25). Peter, however, would not allow Cornelius to cross the line from cordiality to worship. "But Peter lifted him up, saying, 'Stand up; I myself am also a man'" (Acts 10:26).

In most cases, praising or exalting a certain human being may be exaggerated, misguided, or even sinful, but this should not be confused with idolatry. I recently read a criticism of a certain church which claimed that the parishoners, by following their leader blindly, were worshiping their pastor and were committing idolatry. This is another way that idolatry can be trivialized.

"Heil, Hitler!"

A clear example of crossing the line was the unconditional devotion that many Germans gave to Hitler during the time of the Third Reich. Shouting "Heil, Hitler!," and referring to him as "der Fuehrer" (meaning "the Lord") goes much too far. The stiff-armed salute was the equivalent body language of bowing down in worship. The Apostle Peter never would have permitted it.

North Korea's Kim Il Sung Cult

A more contemporary case of worshiping a human being is currently occurring in North Korea. Even when he was alive, Kim Il Sung was worshiped as an omniscient, omnipotent, and omnipresent god. People bowed down to his huge statue. Now, not only idols, but his body itself lying in a glass case, is worshiped by the people. A strict ritual has developed. When entering the room where Kim's body lies, one must first bow

---

*Pledge allegiance to the devil
and you will end up doing
the works of the devil.*

---

down before a white statue of him. Then a visitor must bow at the foot of the glass case, walk to his right side, to his head side, and to his left side, bowing at each place. A visit to the tomb requires no fewer than five acts of worship.

When visitors go into the Kim Il Sung memorial museum in Mt. Myo Hyang, they are led through a maze of 150,000 items given to Kim by visiting heads of state, and they are then ushered into the lead statue room. The statue, a life-sized image, was so remarkably crafted by the Chinese that it is eerily life-like. In describing what happens there, Pastor David Sang-Bok Kim says, "You stand there in front of his image with perfect lighting and background music, and you are told to bow down to pay homage once again."[2]

This is hard-core idolatry. It is substantially different from an American audience standing up in respect as the President walks into a room to the tune of "Hail to the Chief." How dangerous is it? David Kim says, "Would God be pleased with this new cult? Could there be any relationship between the strong idol worship and the current economic decline of North Korea's system? Many believe there is! North Korea needs deliverance."[3]

What Does "To Worship" Mean?

Trivializers of idolatry tend to say things like, "he worships his job" or "she worships her child," or "they worship their mountain cabin." Why do the trivializers do this? In my dictionary, the seventh definition of "worship" is: "7. To feel an adoring reverence for any person or thing." In that sense, it could fit. But that is not the *biblical* use of the term "to worship." The biblical use is more in tune with dictionary definition number one "1. Reverent honor or homage paid to God or a sacred personage or to any object regarded as sacred." Jobs and children and mountain cabins do not fit this meaning.

The Greek word for worship is *proskyneo*, to kiss. The most visible sign of worship is body language, most generally indicating obeisance by bowing, kneeling, or prostrating oneself before the one worshiped. Such an act signifies the worshiper submitting to the will of the one worshiped.

A Fiery Furnace is Better than Misdirected Worship

God takes this act of worship very seriously. King Nebuchadnezzar commanded Daniel and his friends to worship the gold image that he had made, but they refused to do so at the risk of their lives. The price for not worshiping was capital punishment in the furnace. But Daniel said, "Our God whom we serve is able to deliver us from the burning fiery furnace, and He will deliver us from your hand, O king. But if not, let it be known to you, O king, that we do not serve your gods, nor will we worship the gold image which you have set up" (Dan. 3:17-18). Daniel understood worship, and he understood hard-core idolatry. The rest is history.

The *Dictionary of New Testament Theology* says, "[a person's] worship shows who his god is, whether it be the true God, or idols, demons, even Satan himself." When we talk about idolatry, we are talking about those who submit themselves to a spiritual being who is considered, in the mind of the worshiper, a rival to God or a substitute for God or kinder than God. Many people who profess to be Christians in Africa or Asia or to a lesser extent in America will swiftly switch their affection and worship to other spiritual beings if they perceive that the true God is not answering their prayers quickly enough. This is hard-core idolatry. They do not do the same for mountain cabins. Let's be clear on the difference.

Hard-Core Idolatry
Produces Soft-Core Idolatry

Sins in general that fall into our category of soft-core idolatry are often produced by hard-core idolatry. There is a relationship between the two. Those who give obeisance to demonic beings will eventually do their will. Joshua said, "choose you this day whom you will serve." If you choose to serve the kingdom of darkness, you will naturally do the works of the kingdom of darkness.

A good understanding of this comes from Ezekiel 22, a

word of God's judgment on Jerusalem. God said, "The city sheds blood in her own midst, that her time may come; and she makes idols within herself to defile herself. You have become guilty by the blood which you have shed, and have defiled yourself with the idols which you have made" (Ezek. 22:3-4).

What was the result of this hard-core idolatry that involved even blood sacrifice? Some of the outcomes listed in the chapter are:

♦ Dishonoring father and mother (v. 7).

♦ Profaning the Sabbath (v. 8).

♦ Illicit sex (vv. 9-11).

♦ Greed and taking bribes (vv. 12-13).

Soft-core idolatry, such as illicit sex, should not be regarded as "idolatry" (greed, or Mammon, is an exception as I have explained). But it is clear that they are produced by hard-core idolatry, worshiping spiritual beings that are rivals to the true God. Pledge allegiance to the devil and you will end up doing the works of the devil.

Notes

[1] See, for example, *Colossians and Philemon* by Ralph P. Martin (Grand Rapids MI: Wm. B. Eerdmans Publishing Company, 1973), p.104.

[2] David Sang-Bok Kim, "The Unification of Korea from a Christian Perspective," *Korean Torch for World Missions*, Spring 1997, p. 4.

[3] Ibid.

CHAPTER FOUR

But Idols Are Powerless!

I mentioned earlier that one of Satan's major tactics to trivialize idolatry is to make us think that there is no substance to it. For example, referring to idolatry as "superstition" is nothing less than an outward symptom that we have allowed the devil to deceive us. My dictionary says that "superstition" means "irrational belief." In other words, if you believe that idolatry is superstition, you are suggesting that it is just a figment of someone's imagination, and if they were a bit more intelligent they would know that there is nothing really there. This is a serious mistake, because there *is* something there. Something that can seriously harm you.

Using Scripture to Deceive

When Satan met Jesus to tempt Him in the wilderness, he

tried to defeat Jesus by using Scripture. He does the same with trivializing idolatry. He tries to get us to fixate on certain passages of Scripture which, standing alone, can easily blind us to the full truth. Here are two Bible passages that he uses to bring misunderstanding to the true nature of idolatry, one from the Old Testament and one from the New Testament:

♦ Do not learn the way of the Gentiles . . . For one cuts a tree from the forest, the work of the hands of the workman, with the ax. They decorate it with silver and gold; they fasten it with nails and hammers so that it will not topple. They are upright, like a palm tree, and they cannot speak; they must be carried, because they cannot go by themselves. Do not be afraid of them, for they cannot do evil, nor can they do any good (Jer. 10:2-5).

♦ We know that an idol is nothing in the world, and that there is no other God but one (1 Cor. 8:4).

Both of these are descriptions of the *visible* world, not of the *invisible* world. The idols that we see with our eyes have no intrinsic power whatsoever. They are inanimate objects. What does have power, however, is the demonic spirit or spirits who attach themselves to a certain idol and who receive worship as people bow down before the idol or whatever object the demons draw them to. For example, Hawaiians bow down before the volcano Kiluea. That volcano has no power over those people, nor can it receive worship. But behind the volcano in the invisible world is the goddess Pele who is receiving the worship and deceiving the people into thinking that the volcano itself has some supernatural power. The upshot is that this territorial spirit uses her power, which definitely is real, to keep lost souls from receiving the gospel of Christ.

Relating the Invisible to the Visible

Both of these biblical passages explain this difference between the visible and the invisible world if we go on to read a bit more and if we do not stop where Satan desires us to stop. An important principle of biblical interpretation is to understand each Scripture in its context.

In Jeremiah, for example, we have already seen that God accuses His people of committing adultery with stones and trees. It could also be said that Hawaiians commit adultery with a volcano. It is obvious, however, that inanimate rocks, trees and volcanoes do not commit literal, physical adultery in the visible world. That is why Jeremiah goes on, in the same chapter (Jeremiah 3), to explain what is happening in the invisible world. "[You] have scattered your charms to *alien deities* under every green tree" (Jer. 3:13). God sees Hawaiians at the volcano committing spiritual adultery with Pele, and He hates it because He is a jealous God.

Likewise, the Apostle Paul spells out the difference between the visible and the invisible worlds. If we do not stop with 1 Corinthians 8, but if we go on to Chapter 10, we read: "What am I saying then? That an idol is anything, or what is offered to idols is anything? [Obviously not!] But I say that the things which the Gentiles sacrifice they sacrifice to demons and not to God, and I do not want you to have fellowship with demons" (1 Cor. 10:19-20). The danger is not the idol, which is powerless, but the demon associated with the idol, who *is* powerful and who is up to all kinds of mischief.

"The First and Great Commandment"

I first heard Mike Jacobs mention that hard-core idolatry is directly related to what Jesus called "the first and great commandment," that is, "You shall love the Lord your God with all your heart, with all your soul, and with all your mind" (Mt. 22:37-38). Jesus quoted this from Deuteronomy 6 where Moses was giving God's instructions to the children of Israel as they were about to go into the Promised Land. There the commandment was preceded by: "Hear, O Israel: The Lord our God, the Lord is one!" (Deut. 6:4). The point was that they were to serve the true God, and Him only.

God knew they would be tempted by the powerful territorial spirits who had claimed control of the lands over the Jordan for centuries, so He gave them one of the clearest warnings in the Bible. He told Israel not to marry into the people groups in Canaan. Why? "For they will turn your sons away

---

The essence of idolatry is establishing relationships of different kinds and at different levels with personalities in the invisible world.

---

from following Me, to serve other gods; so the anger of the Lord will be aroused against you and destroy you suddenly" (Deut. 7:4). Once again, these are the words of a jealous God who will not tolerate spiritual adultery.

But the gods—the demonic principalities in the invisible world who wanted to be rivals to God—were tangibly honored by material things in the visible world. That is why God goes on to tell them what overt and aggressive action they should take to avoid the pitfall of idolatry: "You shall destroy their altars, and break down their sacred pillars, and cut down their wooden images, and burn their carved images with fire" (Deut. 7:5). In other words, our action in the visible world helps to prevent unholy relationships in the invisible world.

If we, therefore, desire to keep Jesus' "first and great commandment," we must not tolerate hard-core idolatry in any form in our midst, and we must get rid of visible objects which provoke it.

Demons and Idols in the Old Testament

One reason that some Christian leaders are fuzzy on these matters is that, whereas idolatry is dealt with extensively in the Old Testament, demons are not. Before Jesus died on the cross, defeated the devil, and cleansed the heavens causing Satan to fall to earth, God's people did not have much power in combating demons. The ministry of deliverance was rare before the coming of Jesus, but common afterwards. That is why the Pharisees were so astonished at Jesus' authority over demons. Therefore, the connection between the work of demons and hard-core idolatry was not clearly spelled out in the Old Testament. Many of our conclusions come from connecting the various pieces of the relevant biblical data, rather than from a systematic biblical explanation.

In the Old Testament we find a total of only four references to "demons." Each of the four is in the context of making sacrifices to demons, and it is the sacrifices which release the blood of the victim that empower the demons:

- ◆ "They served their idols, which became a snare to them. They even sacrificed their sons and their daughters to demons" (Psa. 106:36-37).

- ◆ "They sacrificed to demons, not to God, to gods they did not know" (Deut. 32:17).

- ◆ "Then [Rehoboam] appointed for himself priests for the high places, for the demons, and the calf idols which he had made" (2 Chron. 11:15).

- ◆ "They shall no more offer their sacrifices to demons, after whom they have played the harlot" (Lev. 17:7).

Given the fact that those are the only mentions of demons in the Old Testament, any confusion on how demons relate to idols is somewhat understandable. Things become much clearer in 1 Corinthians where Paul carefully explains that sacrificing to idols is serving the demonic powers behind the idols.

The Virgin Mary and Maximón

There have been numerous reports, for example, of statues of the Virgin Mary crying tears. There is no need to deny that such a thing might and probably does happen. So how do we explain it? Wooden or stone statues cannot cry. They are powerless to shed tears. Where, then, do the tears come from? They come from the spiritual being in the world of darkness who has become attached to or associated with that idol. To postulate that the spiritual being might be God or God's representative cannot stand up to the light of what God thinks of idols: "You shall not make for yourself any carved image" (Exo. 20:4). The tears are produced by a demonic spirit bent on deceiving people to commit hard-core idolatry.

Similarly, in the highlands of Guatemala one of the most powerful territorial spirits is named Maximón. He is so powerful that his wooden idol (which is nothing in itself, as Jeremiah and Paul would say) has been known to puff on lighted cigars placed in his mouth. Neither tears nor cigar smoke can come from a piece of wood or stone, so we know that some spiritual being other than God is trying to draw people into its sphere of power and control.

This is so important that if we call sports cars or professional football or our jobs or sex or fine dining or education or technology or any such thing "idols," we can easily fail to recognize real idols when we see them. When the word "idol" appears in the Bible, it refers to none of the above. The *Dictionary of New Testament Theology* says that "idol" (Greek *eidolon*) "refers *without exception* to the images of the heathen gods and the deities represented by them" (emphasis mine).[1]

Idolatry Without Idols?

The definition of idolatry that I suggested near the beginning of this book intentionally did not mention the use of idols in the visible world. That is because the *essence* of idolatry is establishing relationships of different kinds and at different levels with personalities in the invisible world. It is violating the first commandment, "You shall have no other gods before me." There can be hard-core idolatry without literal idols as we see in Islam. Muslims do not bow down before idols, but they do pledge their allegiance to and serve Allah, a rival to God.

However, breaking the first commandment is more often than not accompanied by breaking the second commandment which forbids making and bowing down to graven images. Paul affirms this in Romans 1, where he laments that so many people have chosen not to glorify God as God, but rather they "changed the glory of the incorruptible God into an image made like corruptible man—and birds and four-footed beasts and creeping things" (Rom. 1:23). And in Acts 17 he says that perverse people "think that the Divine Nature is like gold or silver or stone, something shaped by art and man's devising" (Acts 17:29). They prefer worshiping the *creature*, such as the devil and demonic spirits, rather than the *Creator*. It can be done with or without material idols.

Notes

[1] W. Mundle, "Image, Idol, Imprint, Example," *The New International Dictionary of New Testament Theology*, Colin Brown, ed. (Grand Rapids MI: Zondervan Publishing House, 1976), Vol. 2, p. 284.

CHAPTER FIVE

IDOLATRY NEXT DOOR

For many Christians, the actual practice of idolatry seems extremely remote. Some might say, "They may do it in Taiwan or Nepal or Haiti or Nigeria, but not in my city. I know many people involved in soft-core idolatry, but not in hard-core idolatry as it is described here." Think again. Real, outright idolatry is more pervasive in our cities and neighborhoods than most Christians think. Without understanding it and dealing with it, efforts to take our cities for God will not be nearly as effective as they should be.

I hate to report it, but people who describe themselves as "Christian" are all too frequently involved in idolatry either consciously or unconsciously. However, not all Christians are. I am currently involved with a large number of evangelical Christian leaders on a personal basis. I know them quite well. I would be surprised, but not incredulous, to learn that one of my leader friends might have been discovered dabbling in

internet pornography or cheating on their income tax or abus-
ing their spouse or padding their expense account or raising
funds illegally. But I would almost bet my house that none of
them is involved in hard-core idolatry. Collectively, the fear
of God is in us and nothing could seduce us into spiritual adultery by forcing us to honor in any way a supernatural demonic
being other than God. The closest that any of us might come
would probably be the temptation to serve Mammon, and I,
for one, pray against that temptation every single morning.

However, I would not be at all surprised to learn that some
other so-called "Christian" leaders out there could actually
be into hard-core idolatry of one kind or another. We might
be shocked if we knew how many individuals who love God,

---

*I am convinced that idolatry in the church can
be a major deterrent to the revival that God
wants to pour out over us and over our cities.*

---

who go to church, who give generously, and who affirm the
Ten Commandments are nevertheless violating the first two
commandments. This is extremely dangerous to us person-
ally. It also imperils our families and it neutralizes our effectiveness in moving out with the army of God into our cities
and beyond. If we get in touch with the supernatural world
through witch doctors, fortune tellers, horoscopes, psychics,
Freemasonry, New Age, good luck charms, palm reading, ESP,
tarot cards, Ouija boards or any such thing, we are committing spiritual adultery, and we can no more expect to escape
the judgment of God than Israel could when they were involved with their forms of idolatry.

Graven Images in Churches?

Some "Christian" churches even contain graven images before which people are allowed to bow, to make obeisance, to light candles, to kiss, to burn incense, to leave gifts, and to otherwise worship and give honor to spirit beings represented by those idols. All this is a tool of the enemy to deceive people and to keep them from finding the true God and being saved.

I realize that many Christian people do this ignorantly, and, if we cannot persuade them that they should change their ways, the best we can do is to pray that God will somehow have mercy on them even though they are committing the sin that He hates the most. I am convinced that this idolatry in the church can be a major deterrent to the revival that God wants to pour out over us and over our cities.

Idolaters in Our Cities

Most of the world's non-Christians are overtly idolatrous. They believe that there is supernatural power in the invisible world, and they do whatever it takes to draw on that power for blessing or for protection. There are some who are true secularists or rationalists or atheists or agnostics or skeptics or humanists, and who, thereby, are not interested in being in touch with a world they cannot see or feel. But they are a small minority of the human race. In our American cities we find numerous devotees to Eastern Religions, Voodoo, Santería, Islam, goddess worship, covens, Wicca, spirit guides, New Age, nature worship, native spirituality, and the like. Events such as the Mardi Gras and Halloween are not colorful, benign, cultural exhibitions, but scheduled and intentional transactions with the demonic realm, and invitations to hard-core idolatry.

One of the reasons that we have not been very effective in evangelizing these people in our cities is that we have not realized the necessity of a power encounter on one level or another. So long as we think that the idols that Buddhists worship are just superstition and that they have no power, but that our real idols are things like overeating and too much television, we have one hand tied behind our back when we reach out to our Buddhist neighbors. The fact of the matter is that these idols, or more precisely the demonic powers attached to them, do have impressive power, and Satan wants to keep us as ignorant of this power as possible. Make no mistake about it. Satan is not a "toothless lion!" If he were, there wouldn't be as many people in hell as there are.

Kublai Khan:
Almost, But Not Quite!

Let me illustrate this, and conclude the chapter, with a little-known story of Marco Polo's friendship with the notorious Mongolian despot, Kublai Khan in the thirteenth century. Marco Polo was an Italian merchant, not a missionary, but nevertheless he and his brothers represented Christianity to Kublai Khan in such a way that the Mongol deeply respected the Christian faith, at one point publicly kissing the Bible. He even seriously considered becoming a Christian. The major reason that he decided not to convert was directly related to hard-core idolatry.

Marco Polo quotes Kublai Khan in *The Travels of Marco Polo* as follows: "Wherefore should I become a Christian? You yourselves must perceive that the Christians of [your] countries are ignorant, inefficient persons, who do not possess the faculty of performing anything [miraculous]; whereas you see that the idolaters can do whatever they will. When I sit at a table the cups that were in the middle of the hall come to me filled with wine and other beverage, spontaneously and without being touched by human hand, and I drink from them. They have the power of controlling bad weather . . ."

"Should I become a convert to the faith of Christ, and profess myself a Christian, the nobles of my court and other persons who do not incline to that religion will ask me what sufficient motives have caused me to receive baptism, and to embrace Christianity. 'What extraordinary powers,' they will say, 'what miracles have been displayed by its ministers? Whereas the idolaters declare that what they exhibit is performed through their own sanctity, and the influence of their idols.' To this I shall not know what answer to make, and I shall be considered by them as laboring under a grievous error; whilst the idolaters, who by means of their profound art can effect such wonders, may without difficulty compass my death."

Marco Polo's sobering commentary is: "From this discourse it must be evident that if the Pope had sent out persons duly qualified to preach the gospel, the grand khan would have embraced Christianity, for which, it is certainly known, he had a strong predilection."[1]

Standing in the Gap

Recognizing and understanding the idolatry of what was then called Cathay, now China, might have turned the tide of history dramatically. That is in the past, but the same applies to our cities and nations and people groups today. God has infinitely more power than the spirits who operate through idols.

He has chosen to release that power as His people stand in the gap with powerful prayer and who go to the front lines with the full armor of God, not loving their lives to the death.

As we strategize taking our cities for God, we will do well to face the facts of hard-core idolatry, both within the church and in the world. When we pray against hard-core idolatry and when we aggressively move out to combat it in the power and anointing of the Holy Spirit, we can see barriers fall and the harvest ripen for soul-winning efforts. If we do this, we can be sure that we are acting according to God's will because we are taking a stand against the sin that God hates the most.

Notes

[1] Marco Polo, The Travels of Marco Polo (London, England: J.M. Dent & Sons Ltd., 1908), Book II, Chapter II, pp. 159-160.

CHAPTER SIX

Let's Do Something About It!

Most of my Christian friends are saying that they would like to see their cities transformed. Few of them would need to be convinced that what we are seeing all around us, day in and day out, seems to be resulting much more from the activities of the forces of darkness than from the kingdom of God in our midst.

Taking Our Cities for God

Is there something we can do about this? We must begin by praying, as Jesus instructed us to do: "Thy kingdom come, Thy will be done on earth as it is in heaven." But we cannot stop there, because a major way that God has chosen to answer our prayers and manifest His kingdom in our communities is to use Christian people as His front-line agents in bringing it about. Are we ready for Him to use us?

Ever since John Dawson published his book, *Taking Our Cities for God* (Creation House) in 1989, the body of Christ has been diligently seeking to understand and to apply the different means that God has been providing us to take our cities. We have come a long way, and many wonderful things have been happening. But few of us would be able to say, "Yes, we have taken our city for God! It is transformed! God's kingdom now far overshadows the kingdom of darkness in our city!"

Why? Why, after years of exponentially increased prayer, of high-quality books and articles on city-taking, of ministries that have come into our cities with well-attended conferences,

---

The finest of our leaders may competently apply all the excellent insights that God has given us for city transformation over the last few years on the highest levels in our cities, but if we do not also deal a significant and simultaneous blow to idolatry, we will not see our dream for city transformation come true.

---

of revival signs in city after city, of pastors' prayer summits, of leaders gathering in large numbers for annual Fasting & Prayer events, of Marches for Jesus, of organized prayerwalking, of massive Promise Keepers' public repentance, of powerful and motivating sermons from our pulpits, and of many other exemplary corporate Christian activities have we seen such relatively scant progress? Several leaders, myself included, have been agonizing over this question for months. Happily, some promising answers are emerging which I believe will help us, by the grace of God, begin to see the breakthroughs that both God and we earnestly desire.

It has only been fairly recently that the Lord has been impressing on me the urgent need to deal aggressively with idolatry if we ever expect to see our cities transformed. If you read the literature that has been coming out on the subject, you will see that this crucial issue has been largely overlooked. The major reason for this, in all probability, is that few of us have really understood the nature of hard-core idolatry, and that is why I am writing this book. Let's get our thinking straight on idolatry, and let's do something about it!

Dealing a Blow
to Idolatry in Our City

This leads into one of the strongest statements I will make in this book: *The finest of our leaders may competently apply all the excellent insights that God has given us for city transformation over the last few years on the highest levels in our cities, but if we do not also deal a significant and simultaneous blow to idolatry, we will not see our dream for city transformation come true.*

The reason I dare to make such a bold statement is that the Bible is so clear about the way that God refuses to move in the way He desires to move if the pathway is clogged with idols.

Take, for example, Jacob. God had called Abraham out of the matrix of sun-goddess worship in Ur and Haran, and Abraham had pledged his total allegiance to the Lord. Isaac followed him, and then Jacob, who was to give birth to the tribes of Israel. But, by that time, through household servants or in-laws or other means, idolatry had crept into Jacob's household. God was ready to take Jacob to a new level in Bethel where He would change his name to Israel and promise him that "a nation and a company of nations shall proceed from you, and kings shall come from your body" (Gen. 35:11).

"Put Away Foreign Gods!"

But the prerequisite for God's will to be accomplished was to abolish the idolatry in their midst. Jacob obeyed. "Jacob said to his household and to all that were with him, 'Put away the foreign gods [i.e., idols] that are among you, purify yourselves, and change your garments. Then let us arise and go up to Bethel; and I will make an altar there to God" (Gen. 35:2-3). This was a radical demand, but there was no question that it had to be done if Jacob's household was to be everything God wanted them to be. "So they gave Jacob all the foreign gods which were in their hands, and all their earrings which were in their ears" (Gen. 35: 4).

What happened? "And they journeyed, and the terror of God was upon the cities that were all around them, and they did not pursue the sons of Jacob" (Gen. 35:5). The hand of God was definitely on them so powerfully that they enjoyed total protection from potential enemies. Getting rid of their idols made all the difference in the world.

What About Jewelry?

Notice that items of jewelry entered the picture. They turned their *earrings* over to Jacob. Why would they do this? It is not because God frowns on the use of decorative jewelry. But there was something about those particular earrings that were giving honor to foreign gods, namely certain demonic spirits, and not to God. In other words, the earrings were idols. As we have seen, honoring those spirits by glorifying them through ornaments is a way of committing spiritual adultery, and God is a jealous God. He simply will not put up with it.

An example occurs to me. Back a few years ago when I was teaching my adult Sunday School class in Lake Avenue Congregational Church in Pasadena, California, we prayed for the sick on a regular basis. One Sunday morning a class member brought a friend who had been suffering for months from a chronic headache that would not go away no matter what. I prayed for her in my normal way and I saw certain things happen which led me to believe that she would be healed. But when I finished, the headache was still there.

Then God drew my attention to a piece of jewelry—a pendant around her neck which had a graven image of the Queen of Heaven in the form of a counterfeit Virgin Mary. "Do you always wear that?" I asked her. "Yes," she replied, "I have worn it for years. I never take it off." So I did what Jacob might have done, and said, "Well, take it off now!" She looked shocked! She said, "I could never take that off. I love her and she loves me. She takes care of me." I said, "She isn't taking care of your headache very well, is she? It's your choice. Take off that medal and get rid of your headache, or leave it on and keep the headache." I turned as if to go, but she told me to wait. I could see that she was agonizing, but finally with trembling hands, she took it off and put it on the table. I prayed again, and the headache left for the first time in months!

Then I said, "Do you want me to take that necklace?" Another long pause. "No," she said, "I'll take care of it." So she picked it up and put it in her purse. I never saw her again, but I could almost guarantee that if she had decided to put that idol back on her neck, the headache would have been back.

Neutralizing the Power of the Philistines

Israel had been taking too many hits from their arch-enemies, the Philistines. The problem? Israel was committing idolatry! So at a critical moment, their leader, Samuel, said, "If you return to the Lord with all your hearts, then put away the foreign gods and the Ashtoreths [i.e., the idols] from among you, and prepare your hearts for the Lord, and serve Him only; and He will deliver you from the Philistines" (1 Sam. 7:3). Once again, God's people were missing God's best for them because they had a dual allegiance—to God and to their idols. God does not allow you to have it both ways.

Fortunately, when they realized the error of their ways, they repented for their sin and they decided to give their full allegiance to God. "So the children of Israel put away the Baals and the Ashtoreths, and served the Lord only" (1 Sam. 7:4). As a result, "the Philistines were subdued, and they did not come any more into the territory of Israel" (1 Sam. 7:13). I believe that we could see similar results in our cities today if we decided to deal decisively with hard-core idolatry and thus rid our cities of our contemporary Baals and Ashtoreths.

How Strong Can Idols Be? Paul Knows!

One of the best examples of the power of idolatry to block the entrance of the kingdom of God into a city is Paul's experience in Athens. Paul reaped abundant spiritual fruit in Thessalonica and Berea before he went to Athens, and he reaped abundant fruit in Corinth and Ephesus after he left Athens. But in Athens he saw very few converts and he left no church behind that we hear anything more about. What had blocked Paul's ministry there? Idolatry! "[Paul's] spirit was provoked within him when he saw that the city was given over to idols" (Acts 17:16). True, cities like Thessalonica, Berea, Corinth, and Ephesus had their share of idols. But not like Athens. Athens was notable in ancient literature for its unusually extravagant idolatry. Athens was called a forest of idols. Some said that it was easier to find a god in Athens than a human being. One estimate calculated that the city of Athens housed more idols than all the rest of Greece combined!

How hard did Paul try to take Athens for Christ? As hard as he could. In fact, the consensus among homiletics professors is that Paul preached his most brilliant sermon in Athens—the Sermon on Mars Hill. But the forces of darkness, led by the goddess Athena, had built almost impenetrable defenses against the gospel through festivals, pilgrimages, rituals, unholy sculptures, ornate demonic temples, blood sacrifices, altars inside and outside of every home, sacred pillars, and public invitations by civic officials for the demonic principalities to maintain possession of their city. Paul had met his match in the spiritual realm. That is how powerful hard-core idolatry can be![1]

If Paul found the idolatry of Athens so formidable an obstacle, it should not surprise us that our cities today are so hard to take for the kingdom. I frankly doubt if any American city is as thoroughly idolatrous as Athens was, but that does not mean that idolatry is not a powerful barrier to the gospel of the kingdom in virtually every one of our cities. Paul broke through the idolatry in many other cities, and so can we.

San La Muerte of Resistencia

Resistencia, Argentina, while probably not as idolatrous as
Athens, had given itself over as a playground for several powerful demonic principalities. Resistencia was the target of one
of the first city-taking efforts in the 1990s, led by Ed Silvoso of
Harvest Evangelism. My wife, Doris, and I, along with Cindy
Jacobs and several others, joined Silvoso in a three-year effort
to see a true spiritual breakthrough in Resistencia beginning
in 1990.

The highest-ranking spirit in that Northern Argentina city
of 400,000 was San La Muerte, literally translated, "St. Death."
Thirteen shrines to St. Death throughout the city offered easy
access for worship to the entire population. His idol was a
skeleton. Why did people worship this spirit? Because he
had promised them a "good death!" It is hard to imagine a
people so hopeless and full of despair that the most they could
hope for down the road was a good death! In fact, many had
miniature idols of San La Muerte surgically implanted in parts
of their bodies, such as under their nipples, so that wherever
they went, San La Muerte would go with them and give them
a good death.

The few Christian pastors of the city joined forces with
Silvoso's team and declared war on San La Muerte and his
cohorts. Open spiritual confrontation was the order of the
day. Multiple strategic events took place in carefully-planned
sequence over a 36-month period. The culmination was to be
a massive public evangelistic campaign, featuring all the leaders of the Argentine revival.

While the city was notoriously and openly idolatrous, it

took some time to recognize the fact that a good bit of this idolatry had spilled over into the body of Christ as well. Many believers were found to be acting like the ancient children of Israel under Samuel—they had their modern counterparts to Israel's Baals and Ashtoreths somewhere on their persons or in their homes.

"Burn the Idols!"

Doris was preparing to travel to Argentina with Cindy Jacobs for the climactic evangelistic campaign. As she was reading Scripture the morning she was to leave, the Holy Spirit told her that in Resistencia they must burn the idols, like the magicians did in Ephesus. Ed Silvoso, Cindy Jacobs and the Resistencia pastors agreed. So the evening before the evangelistic crusade, all the city's believers came together for prayer. The leaders explained how important it would be to do spiritual housecleaning in their homes before they came to the meeting. They began mentioning the kinds of material things that might be bringing honor to the spirits of darkness: pictures, statues, Catholic saints, Books of Mormon, pictures of former lovers, pornographic material, fetishes, drugs, Ouija boards, zodiac charms, good luck symbols, crystals for healing, amulets, talismans, tarot cards, witch dolls, voodoo items, love potions, books of magic, totem poles, certain pieces of jewelry, objects of Freemasonry, horoscopes, gargoyles, native art, foreign souvenirs, and what have you.

The believers agreed to obey God and to cleanse their homes, even if it meant giving up what might have been expensive items. They were to wrap each item in newspaper to protect privacy, and then cast the objects into a 55-gallon drum set before the platform the following night. The drum was heaped to overflowing! They poured gasoline on it and set it on fire. This was a major power encounter, because the witches and warlocks had surrounded the area and done their occult sacrifices, killing animals, burning incense, and sending the most powerful curses they could muster toward the evangelists. When the flames shot up, a woman right behind Doris screamed and manifested a demon, which Doris immediately cast out!

The Fall of San La Muerte

Many unbelievers came to Christ that night, and each one was instructed to go home, do their own spiritual housecleaning, and bring their objects to the bonfire the following night. As this went on, night after night, San La Muerte's power diminished. The breakthrough that the believers had prayed for occurred. Eighteen new churches sprang up, and the evangelical population increased many fold over the next few years.

As if to headline how the aggressive onslaught against idolatry had succeeded, God permitted a spectacular event to occur one week before the evangelistic campaign. Resistencia's high priestess of San La Muerte had been smoking in her bed. She fell asleep, and her bed caught fire. The only things that were consumed by fire were the bed, the woman, and her idol of San La Muerte *located in the next room!* No wonder the city was ready to hear the word of God!

Notes

[1] If readers might be experiencing difficulty with the premise that Paul's ministry could be neutralized by demonic forces, I urge them to read my full exposition of the Athens experience in my commentary on Acts, *Acts of the Holy Spirit* (Regal Books), pp. 424-439.

CHAPTER SEVEN

Spiritual Housecleaning

I'm sure that many by now will have decided that some spiritual housecleaning of our own might be a good thing. But at that point, it becomes quite personal. How do I decide what I should get rid of and what I should keep? Where do we draw the line?

Where Do We Draw the Line?

Doris and I were missionaries in Bolivia for 16 years. We never consciously engaged in any form of hard-core idolatry, although there was a great deal of it going on around us. Our biggest disadvantage was that we had received no instruction on this issue in all of our training, nor did we have access to books like this one. Because of this, we have concluded that the results of our 16 years of strenuous labor produced mediocre results at best. We made many more than our share of naïve mistakes.

We brought one of them home with us. When we set up housekeeping in Pasadena, California, so that I could teach at Fuller Seminary, we used a Bolivian motif to decorate the rooms of our Spanish-style home. It wasn't until the late 1980s that we began understanding a bit about issues such as idolatry and spiritual warfare. Our personal challenge for drawing the line revolved around three artistic household decorations: (1) a souvenir Quechua Indian stone puma that we had purchased in a Bolivian tourist shop, (2) a pair of wooden masks that had been used in Chiquitano Indian pagan ceremonies, and (3) a beautiful pair of carved wooden lamps, fashioned in the image if Inti, the Aymara Indian sun god.

What Do We Destroy?

Through a housecleaning-type prayer time in our home, which I won't describe in detail at the moment, we had discovered that there was an evil spirit who had taken up residence in the puma. So we immediately proceeded to destroy the puma and rebuke the spirit. Then our attention was drawn to the masks on the wall. Although we were not sure whether any spirits were attached to the masks or not, they had nevertheless been used in actual worship of spirits of darkness (hardcore idolatry), so we decided to destroy them as well. Those two decisions were fairly easy. But when we looked at the lamps on our living room end tables, we thought how much we had paid for them, and how exquisite was the handiwork. They did not have a spirit attached like the puma did, nor had they been used in worship as the masks had been. We reasoned that they were just nice, attractive pieces of Bolivian native art. So we decided there would be nothing wrong in keeping them—until Cindy Jacobs first visited our home.

In her very gentle way, Cindy suggested that we might want to pray a bit more about keeping the lamps. We did, and we soon discovered that we had not been asking the right question about the lamps. The question is: *Do they glorify God?* The answer obviously was, "No!" Those lamps had been crafted with no thought of bringing glory to God, but in order to bring glory to a demonic principality named Inti. They, therefore, were idols and they had to go. When we finished this spiritual housecleaning, our home was still quite distinctly decorated with a Bolivian motif. But we had learned how to draw the line—what to keep and what not to keep. The peace of God came upon our home!

Avoiding God's Wrath

We then began to understand more clearly what Paul meant when he described how the wrath of God is released in Romans 1. God's invisible attributes had been reflected in His

*Let's give our total
and undivided allegiance
to the Lord!*

creation in order to glorify Him (see Rom. 1:20). But human beings provoked God's wrath by using His creation to "change the glory of the incorruptible God into an image make like corruptible man—and birds and four-footed beasts and creeping things" (Rom. 1:23). When he was in the idolatrous city of Athens itself, Paul said, "[God] does not dwell in temples made with hands. Nor is He worshiped with men's hands . . . We ought not to think that the Divine Nature is like gold or silver or stone, something shaped by art and man's devising" (Acts 17:24,25,29).

How bad can God's wrath be? Romans 1 says four different times that God gave these idolatrous people up! And Paul's simple advice to the idolaters in Athens was: "[God] now commands all men everywhere to repent" (Acts 17:30).

Let's Get Serious!

So let's get serious! Let's repent. Let's ask God to forgive us for trivializing idolatry. Let's repent of the idolatry that has crept into church after church. Let's honor God by thorough spiritual housecleaning. Let's pray for a spirit of wisdom and revelation as we examine our surroundings for ungodly items. Let's remind each other continually how much God detests spiritual adultery. Let's increase our prayer power for unbelievers in our communities who persist in idolatry. Let's ask God to show His heart to those who bow down or light candles to statues and graven images. Let's be courageous enough to take a stand when it might mean personal rejection by others. Let's give our total and undivided allegiance to the Lord!

If we do as the Thessalonians did, namely turn "to God from idols to serve the living and true God" (1 Thess. 1:9), we can then position ourselves for God to use us in giving Him greater glory, in being the people He wants us to be, in seeing our cities truly transformed, and in releasing God's will to be done on earth as it is in heaven!

SUBJECT INDEX

Ridding Your Home of Spiritual Darkness

Chuck D. Pierce
& Rebecca Wagner Sytsema

Christians are often completely unaware
of how the enemy has gained access to
their homes through what they own.
This practical, easy-to-read book can be
used by any Christian to pray through
their home and property in order to
close the door to the enemy and experience richer spiritual life. Included are
chapters on:

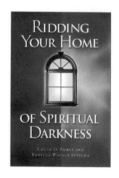

- Understanding spiritual darkness

- Children

- Generational curses

- Spiritual discernment

- Land and property

- A ten-step guide to praying through your home

Christian Living
Paperback • 80p
ISBN 1-58502-008-7 • $7.95

Available at finer bookstores
or by calling toll-free 888-563-5150

Radical Holiness
For Radical Living

C. Peter Wagner

Holiness has long been a topic of
great debate. In this easy-to-read
book, C. Peter Wagner helps bring
clarity to the topic by answering
many questions including:

- Can anyone really live a holy
  life?

- Is there a test of holiness?

- What are the non-negotiable principles for
  radical holiness?

- How much holiness should be required of a
  leader?

For any believer who wants to be everything God
wants them to be, this book will open the way for
them to move to new levels in their Christian
lives. Through radical holiness, readers will learn
to defeat Satan's schemes and enjoy daily victory
in their walk with God!

Christian Living
Paperback • 60p
ISBN 0.9667481.1.5 • $6.95

Available at finer bookstores
or by calling toll-free 888-563-5150

Revival!

It Can Transform Your City

C. Peter Wagner

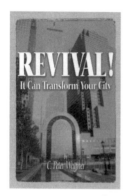

This book takes you beyond city taking to city transformation!

Questions addressed include:

- What exactly is revival?

- Can a city actually be transformed through revival?

- How can Christians move to new levels of spiritual warfare to see revival come?

- What new wineskins is the Holy Spirit using to facilitate revival?

- What steps can be taken to sustain revival in a city?

Discover how the Spirit of God can visibly transform cities through the revival we have been praying for.

Leadership/Spiritual Warfare
Paperback • 63p
ISBN 0.9667481.8.2 • $6.00

Available at finer bookstores
or by calling toll-free 888-563-5150

Seven Power Principles

That I Didn't Learn in Seminary

C. Peter Wagner

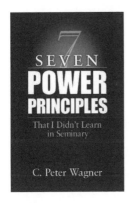

God is moving with power in the world today! In this book, Wagner captures 7 key principles for moving in that power.

"God is alive and active today but the evidence of His activity is often difficult to find in Evangelical seminaries and the churches pastored by seminary graduates. Peter Wagner is a standard-bearer for the growing numbers of Christian leaders and churches that are moving with God beyond the drag of intellectualism. This book is a worthy summary of what God has been teaching many of us since seminary. I pray that God will use it to point the way for many more church leaders to follow the Holy Spirit's guidance beyond what they learned in seminary."

Dr. Charles Kraft
Professor of Anthropology and Intercultural Communication
Fuller Theological Seminary, Pasadena, California

Leadership/Spiritual Warfare
Paperback • 86p
ISBN 1-58502-014-1 • $7.00

Available at finer bookstores
or by calling toll-free 888-563-5150